Published by
Wise Publications
14-15 Berners Street,
London W1T 3LJ, UK

Exclusive Distributors:
Music Sales Limited
Distribution Centre,
Newmarket Road,
Bury St Edmunds,
Suffolk IP33 3YB, UK

Music Sales Pty Limited
20 Resolution Drive,
Caringbah, NSW 2229,
Australia

Order No. AM998756
ISBN 978-1-84938-278-6

Edited by Oliver Miller
Cover design and illustrations
by Lizzie Barrand.

Printed in the EU

www.musicsales.com

Wise Publications
part of The Music Sales Group
London / New York / Paris / Sydney / Copenhagen / Berlin / Madrid / Hong Kong / Tokyo

alice the camel

Verse 1

Alice the camel has five humps,
Alice the camel has five humps,
Alice the camel has five humps,
So go, Alice, go!
Boom, boom, boom!

Verse 2

Alice the camel has four humps,
Alice the camel has four humps,
Alice the camel has four humps,
So go, Alice, go!
Boom, boom, boom!

Verse 3

Alice the camel has three humps,
Alice the camel has three humps,
Alice the camel has three humps,
So go, Alice, go!
Boom, boom, boom!

Verse 4

Alice the camel has two humps,
Alice the camel has two humps,
Alice the camel has two humps,
So go, Alice, go!
Boom, boom, boom!

Verse 5

Alice the camel has one hump,
Alice the camel has one hump,
Alice the camel has one hump,
So go, Alice, go!
Boom, boom, boom!

Verse 6

Alice the camel has no humps,
Alice the camel has no humps,
Alice the camel has no humps,
Now Alice is a horse!

Traditional

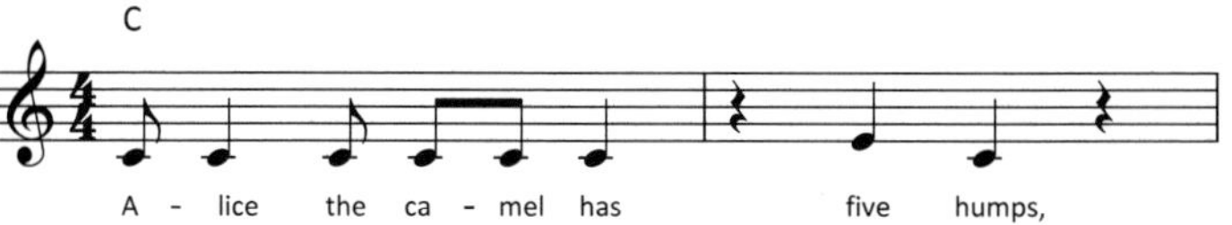
C
A - lice the ca - mel has five humps,

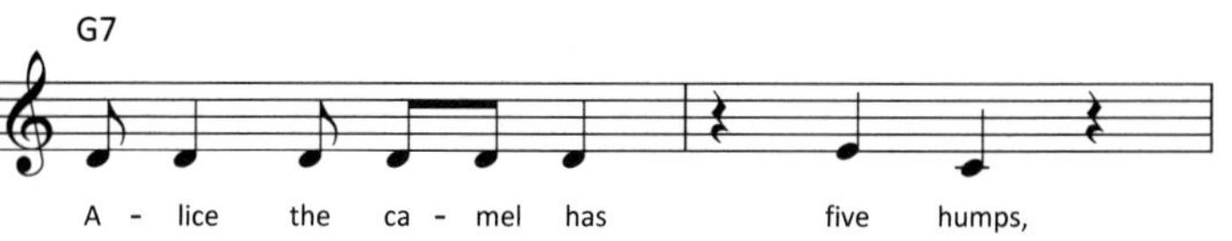
G7
A - lice the ca - mel has five humps,

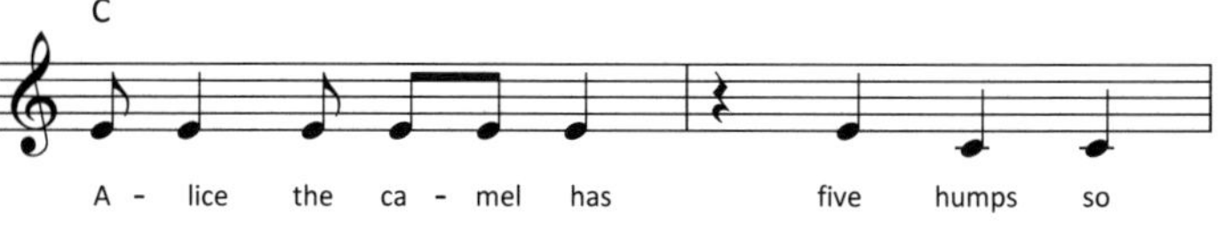
C
A - lice the ca - mel has five humps so

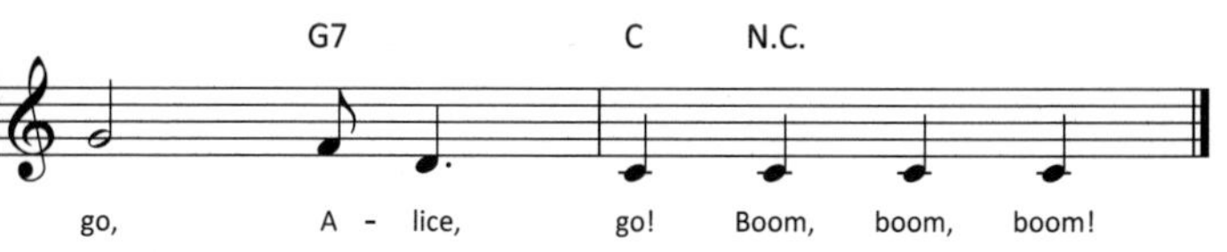
G7
C
N.C.
go, A - lice, go! Boom, boom, boom!

the alphabet song

A - B - C - D - E - F - G
H - I - J - K - L - M - N - O - P
Q - R - S and T - U - V
W - X - Y and Z.
Now you know your A - B - C
You can come and play with me.

Traditional

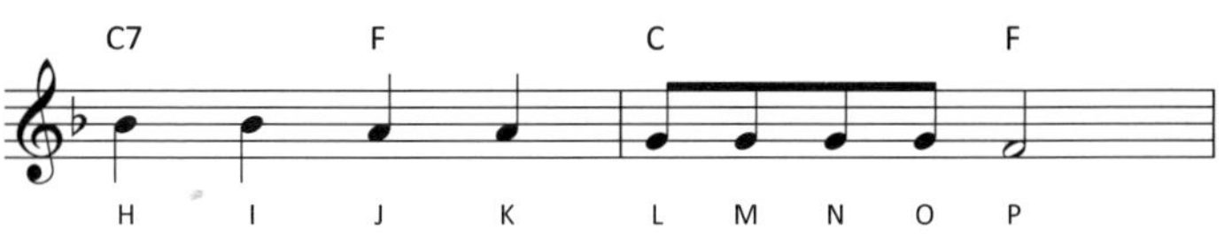

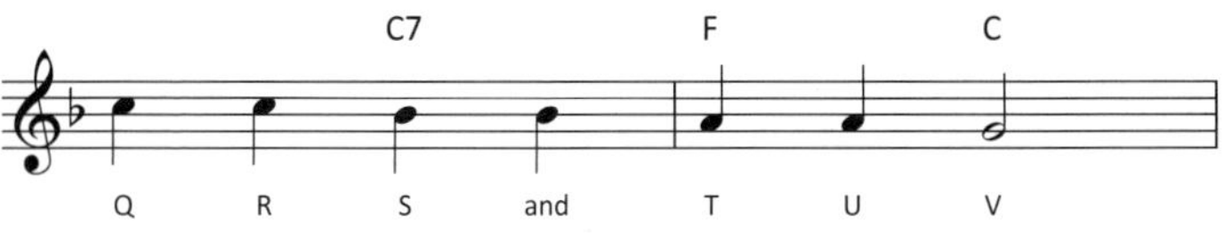

the camptown races

Verse 1

Camptown ladies sing this song,
Doo-dah, doo-dah,
Camptown racetrack five miles long,
Oh, doo-dah day.
Come down there with my hat caved in,
Doo-dah, doo-dah,
Go back home with my pocket full of tin,
Oh, doo-dah-day.

Goin' to run all night, goin' to run all day.
I bet my money on the bobtail nag;
Somebody bet on the bay.

Verse 2

The long-tail filly and the big black hoss,
Doo-dah, doo-dah,
Fly the track and they both cut across,
Oh, doo-dah-day.
The blind hoss shaken in a big mud hole,
Doo-dah, doo-dah,
Can't touch bottom with a ten-foot pole,
Oh, doo-dah-day.

Goin' to run all night, goin' to run all day.
I bet my money on the bobtail nag;
Somebody bet on the bay.

Verse 3

Old muley cow came onto the track,
Doo-dah, doo-dah,
Bobtail fling her over his back,
Oh, doo-dah-day.
Then fly along like a railroad car,
Doo-dah, doo-dah,
Running a race with a shooting star,
Oh, doo-dah-day.

Goin' to run all night, goin' to run all day.
I bet my money on the bobtail nag;
Somebody bet on the bay.

Verse 4

See the flying on a ten-mile heat,
Doo-dah, doo-dah,
'Round the racetrack, then repeat,
Oh, doo-dah-day.
I win my money on a bobtail nag,
Doo-dah, doo-dah,
Keep my money in an old tow bag,
Oh, doo-dah-day.

Goin' to run all night, goin' to run all day.
I bet my money on the bobtail nag;
Somebody bet on the bay.

Words & Music by Stephen Foster

D
A7
Camp - town la - dies sing this song, doo - dah, doo - dah,

D
A7
D
Camp - town race - track five miles long, oh, doo - dah - day.

A7
Come down there with my hat caved in, doo - dah, doo - dah;

D
A7
D
Go back home with my pock - et full of tin, oh, doo - dah - day.

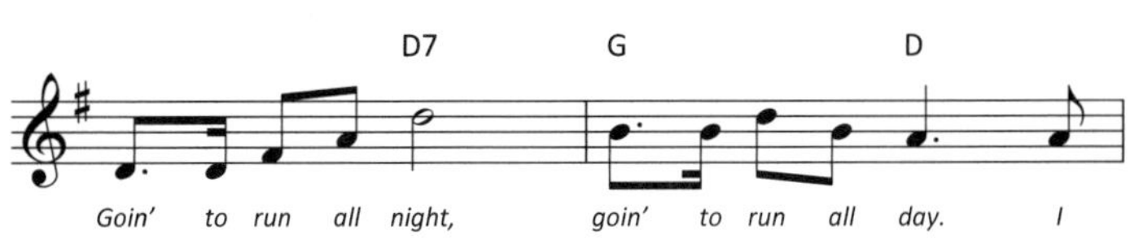
D7
G
D
Goin' to run all night, goin' to run all day. I

A7
D
bet my mon - ey on the bob - tail nag; some - bod - y bet on the bay.

do your ears hang low?

Verse 1
Do your ears hang low?
Do they wobble to and fro?
Can you tie 'em in a knot?
Can you tie 'em in a bow?
Can you throw 'em o'er your shoulder
Like a Continental Soldier?
Do your ears hang low?

Verse 2
Do your ears hang high?
Do they reach up to the sky?
Do they wrinkle when they're wet?
Do they straighten when they're dry?
Can you wave 'em at your neighbour
With an element of flavour?
Do your ears hang high?

Verse 3
Do your ears hang wide?
Do they flap from side to side?
Do they wave in the breeze
From the slightest little sneeze?
Can you soar above the nation
With a feeling of elation?
Do your ears hang wide?

Verse 4
Do your ears fall off
When you give a great big cough?
Do they lie there on the ground
Or bounce up at every sound?
Can you stick them in your pocket
Just like Davy Crocket?
Do your ears fall off?

Verse 5
Does your tongue hang out?
Can you shake it all about?
When you try to tuck it in,
Does it just hang out?
Can you roll it to the ground
With a chink and a pound?
Does your tongue hang out?

Verse 6
Does your nose hang low?
Does it wiggle to and fro?
Can you tie it in a knot?
Can you tie it in a bow?
Can you throw it o'er your shoulder
Like a continental soldier?
Does your nose hang low?

Verse 7
Do your eyes pop out?
Do they bounce all about?
Can you tie them in a knot?
Can you tie them in a bow?
Can you throw them o'er your shoulder
Like a Continental Soldier?
Do your eyes pop out?

Traditional

G
D
Do your ears hang low? Do they wob- ble to and fro? Can you

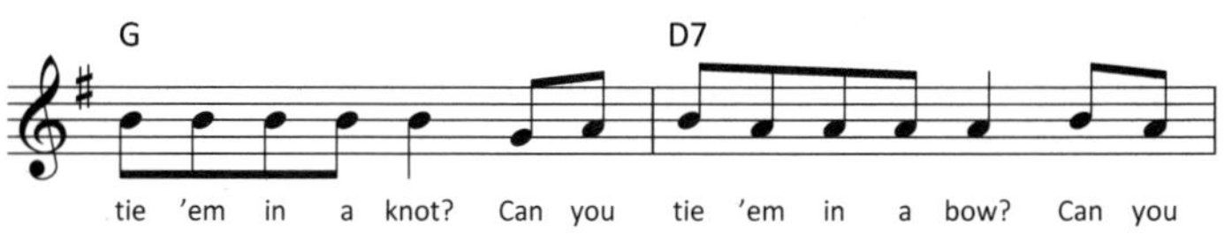
G
D7
tie 'em in a knot? Can you tie 'em in a bow? Can you

G
throw 'em o'er your shoul - der like a

D
D7
G
con - ti - nen - tal sol- dier? Do Your ears hang low?

travel games

Tell A Tale

A story is created by each player saying three words at a time for a continuing dialogue. The first player might begin, "One day in…", the next could continue, "a big house…", the next, "there lived a…", and so on. The story can continue until someone ends it or it is impossible to carry on.

The game can go on for a long time!

Counting Cows

Each player counts all the cows they see from their side of the vehicle. If a cemetery is passed then the player on that side loses all their cows. The person with the most cows at the end of the journey is the winner.

Say What You See

Each player takes it in turns to say what they see out of the vehicle window. You may name one thing at a time without repeating what another player has already mentioned. The game becomes increasingly difficult as more and more things are named.

Silly Animals

By taking the letters from a car number plate, in turn each player comes up with a silly animal name, for example 'BSH' could be Big Smelly Hippopotamus. The first two letters should always be adjectives (words which describe the animal) and the last is the type of animal.

This game could be varied for Silly Places or even Silly Friends!

ging gang goolie

Ging gang goolie goolie goolie goolie watcha
Ging gang goo, ging gang goo.
Ging gang goolie goolie goolie goolie watcha
Ging gang goo, ging gang goo.
Heyla, oh heyla sheyla,
Oh heyla sheyla heyla hoo.
Heyla, oh heyla sheyla,
Oh heyla sheyla heyla hoo.
Shalli walli shalli walli shalli walli shalli walli
Oompah oompah oompah oompah oompah oompah pah.

Try singing this song in a round. The first time through, everyone sings. One group continues to sing 'Oompah', while another group begins the song again. When the second group reaches 'Hayla' the 'Oompah' groups joins in from the same point. When the end is reached the groups split up, as before, only swapping parts.

Traditional

the grand old duke of york

Here is the song with actions included!

Oh, the grand old Duke of York,
He had ten thousand men,
He marched them up to the top of the hill
(Everyone stands up)
And he marched them down again.
(Everyone sits down)
And when they were up, they were up,
(Everyone stands up)
And when they were down, they were down.
(Everyone sits down)
And when they were only half way up
(Everyone stands up half-way)
They were neither up nor down.

Traditional

i know an old lady who swallowed a fly

Verse 1

I know an old lady who swallowed a fly,
I don't know why she swallowed a fly –
Perhaps she'll die!

Verse 2

I know an old lady who swallowed a spider
That wriggled and jiggled and tickled inside her.
She swallowed the spider to catch the fly;
I don't know why she swallowed a fly –
Perhaps she'll die!

Verse 3

I know an old lady who swallowed a bird;
How absurd to swallow a bird.
She swallowed the bird to catch the spider,
She swallowed the spider to catch the fly;
I don't know why she swallowed a fly –
Perhaps she'll die!

Verse 4

I know an old lady who swallowed a cat;
Fancy that to swallow a cat!
She swallowed the cat to catch the bird,
She swallowed the bird to catch the spider,
She swallowed the spider to catch the fly;
I don't know why she swallowed a fly –
Perhaps she'll die!

Verse 5

I know an old lady who swallowed a dog;
What a hog, to swallow a dog.
She swallowed the dog to catch the cat,
She swallowed the cat to catch the bird,
She swallowed the bird to catch the spider,
She swallowed the spider to catch the fly;
I don't know why she swallowed a fly –
Perhaps she'll die!

Verse 6

I know an old lady who swallowed a cow;
I don't know how she swallowed a cow.
She swallowed the cow to catch the dog,
She swallowed the dog to catch the cat,
She swallowed the cat to catch the bird,
She swallowed the bird to catch the spider,
She swallowed the spider to catch the fly;
I don't know why she swallowed a fly –
Perhaps she'll die!

I know an old lady who swallowed a horse...
She's dead, of course!

Traditional

london's burning

London's burning,
London's burning.
Fetch the engines,
Fetch the engines.
Fire! Fire!
Fire! Fire!
Pour on water,
Pour on water.

When you know this song well, you can sing it as a round in 2, 3 or 4 parts. You could even add some instruments like recorders or xylophones, singers could be groups 1 and 3, instruments groups 2 and 4.

Traditional

F
C
Lon - don's burn - ing, Lon - don's burn - ing. Fetch the

F
C
F
C
en - gines, fetch the en - gines. Fire!

F
C
F
C
Fire! Fire! Fire! Pour on

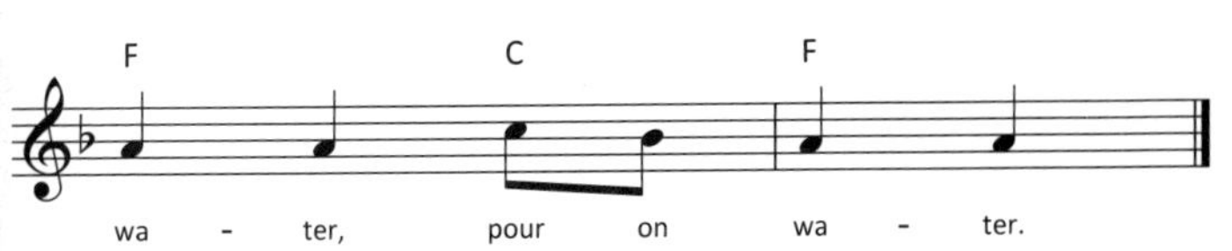
F
C
F
wa - ter, pour on wa - ter.

travel jokes

Did you hear about the red ship and the blue ship that collided?
The survivors were marooned.

What happens when a frog's car breaks down?
It gets toad away.

Glancing into the car, he was astounded to see that the lady who was driving was knitting. Realising that she was oblivious to his flashing lights and siren, the policeman wound down his window, turned on his loudspeaker and yelled, "Pull over!"
"No", the lady yelled back, "It's a scarf!"

What bus crossed the ocean?
Columbus.

Which snakes are found on cars?
Windscreen vipers.

A man standing at a bus stop was eating a hamburger. Next to him stood a lady with her little dog, which became very excited at the smell of the man's supper and began whining and jumping up at him.
"Do you mind if I throw him a bit?" said the man to the lady.
"Not at all," she replied, whereupon the man picked the dog up and threw it over a wall.

What did the jack say to the car?
"Can I give you a lift?"

Who drives away all his customers?
A taxi driver.
"Is everyone in the bus?" asked the driver before he closed the door.
"No," called a lady, "Wait until I get my clothes on."
All the passengers in the bus turned towards
the door to look at the woman.
She got on with a bag full of laundry.
Why did the car judder to a stop when it saw a ghost?
It had a nervous breakdown.
Janet: What's the difference between a cake and a school bus?
Jill: I don't know.
Janet: Then I'm glad I didn't send you to pick up my birthday cake!
What did the bus conductor say to the frog?
"Hop on."
How do eels get around the seabed?
They go by octobus.
My dad is stupid. He thinks a fjord is a Norwegian motor car.
Why did the stupid racing car driver make
ten pit stops during the Grand Prix?
He was asking for directions.
Does this bus stop at the river?
If it doesn't there'll be a very big splash.

merrily we roll along

Merrily we roll along,
Roll along, roll along.
Merrily we roll along
O'er the deep blue sea.

Traditional

G
D
G
Mer - ri - ly we roll a - long, roll a - long, roll a - long.

D
G
Mer - ri - ly we roll a - long o'er the deep blue sea.

nellie the elephant

Cm G7 Cm
1. To Bom - bay a trav - el - ling cir - cus
G D7 G
came. They brought an in - tel - li - gent el - e - phant and
D7 G Cm G7
Nel - lie was her name. One dark
Cm G
night she slipped her i - ron chain and
D7 G Am7 D7
off she ran to Hin - du - stan and was nev - er seen a -
G C
gain. Nel - lie the el - e - phant packed her trunk and
F C Dm7 G7
said good - bye to the cir - cus, off she went with a
Em7 Am D9 D7 G
trum - pet - y trump, trump, trump, trump.
C F
Nel - lie the el - e - phant packed her trunk and bun - dled back to the

Words by Ralph Butler
Music by Peter Hart

C Dm7 G7 Em7 Am
jun - gle. Off she went with a trum - pet - y trump,

Dm7 G7 C F
trump, trump, trump. The head of the herd was

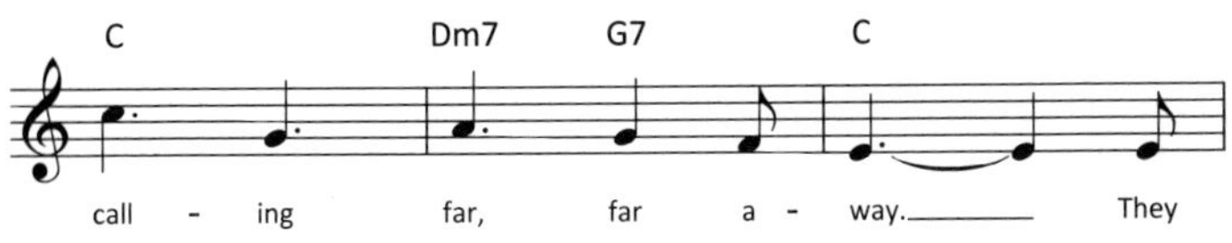
C Dm7 G7 C
call - ing far, far a - way. They

D7 G D7
met one night in the sil - ver light on the road to Man - da -

G C
lay. So, Nel - lie the el - e - phant packed her trunk and

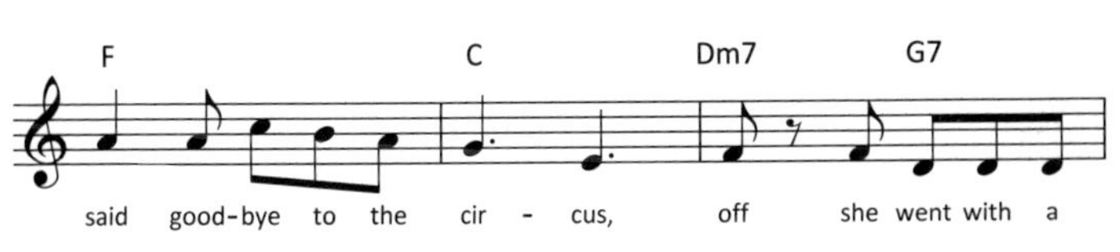
F C Dm7 G7
said good-bye to the cir - cus, off she went with a

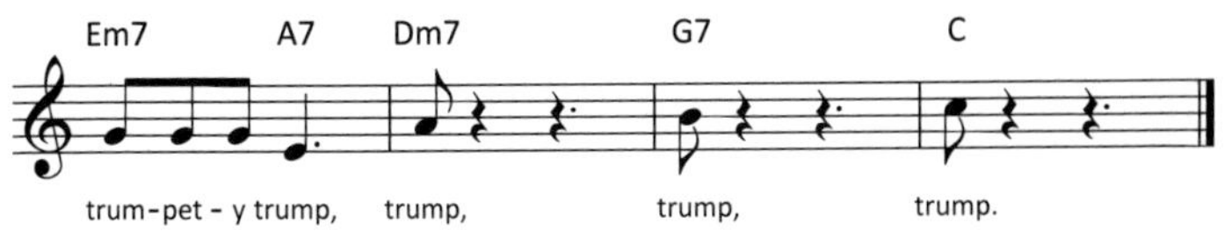
Em7 A7 Dm7 G7 C
trum-pet - y trump, trump, trump, trump.

oh dear! what can the matter be?

Oh dear! What can the matter be?
Dear, dear! What can the matter be?
Oh dear! What can the matter be?
Johnny's so long at the fair.

Verse 1
He promised to buy me a bunch of blue ribbons,
He promised to buy me a bunch of blue ribbons,
He promised to buy me a bunch of blue ribbons
To tie up my bonnie brown hair.

Oh dear! What can the matter be?
Dear, dear! What can the matter be?
Oh dear! What can the matter be?
Johnny's so long at the fair.

Verse 2
He promised to buy me a trinket to please me
And then for a smile, oh, he vowed he would tease me,
He promised to buy me a bunch of blue ribbons
To tie up my bonnie brown hair.

Oh dear! What can the matter be?
Dear, dear! What can the matter be?
Oh dear! What can the matter be?
Johnny's so long at the fair.

Verse 3
He promised to bring me a basket of posies,
A garland of lilies, a gift of red roses,
A little straw hat to set off the blue ribbons
That tie up my bonnie brown hair.

Oh dear! What can the matter be?
Oh dear! What can the matter be?
Oh dear! What can the matter be?
Johnny's so long at the fair.

Traditional

old macdonald

Verse 1
Old MacDonald had a farm,
Ee - eye, ee - eye, oh!
And on that farm he had some chicks,
Ee - eye, ee - eye, oh!
With a chick, chick here
And a chick, chick there.
Here a chick, there a chick,
Everywhere a chick, chick.
Old MacDonald had a farm,
Ee - eye, ee - eye, oh!

Verse 2
Old MacDonald had a farm,
Ee - eye, ee - eye, oh!
And on that farm he had a dog,
Ee - eye, ee - eye, oh!
With a bow, wow here
And a bow, wow there.
Here a bow, there a wow,
Everywhere a bow, wow.
Old MacDonald had a farm,
Ee - eye, ee - eye, oh!

Verse 3
Old MacDonald had a farm,
Ee - eye, ee - eye, oh!
And on that farm he had a pig,
Ee - eye, ee - eye, oh!
With an oink, oink here
And an oink, oink there.
Here an oink, there a oink,
Everywhere a oink, oink.
Old MacDonald had a farm,
Ee - eye, ee - eye, oh!

Verse 4
Old MacDonald had a farm,
Ee - eye, ee - eye, oh!
And on that farm he had a cockerel,
Ee - eye, ee - eye, oh!
With a cock-a-doodle here
And a cock-a-doodle there.
Here a cock-a, there a doodle
Everywhere a cock-a-doodle.
Old MacDonald had a farm,
Ee - eye, ee - eye, oh!

Verse 5
Old MacDonald had a farm,
Ee - eye, ee - eye, oh!
And on that farm he had a turkey,
Ee - eye, ee - eye, oh!
With a gobble, gobble here
And a gobble, gobble there.
Here a gobble, there a gobble,
Everywhere a gobble, gobble.
Old MacDonald had a farm,
Ee - eye, ee - eye, oh!

Verse 6
Old MacDonald had a farm,
Ee - eye, ee - eye, oh!
And on that farm he had a cat,
Ee - eye, ee - eye, oh!
With a meow, meow here
And a meow, meow there.
Here a meow, there a meow,
Everywhere a meow, meow.
Old MacDonald had a farm,
Ee - eye, ee - eye, oh!

Verse 7
Old MacDonald had a farm,
Ee - eye, ee - eye, oh!
And on that farm he had a horse,
Ee - eye, ee - eye, oh!
With a neigh, neigh here
And a neigh, neigh there.
Here a neigh, there a neigh,
Everywhere a neigh, neigh.
Old MacDonald had a farm,
Ee - eye, ee - eye, oh!

Verse 8
Old MacDonald had a farm,
Ee - eye, ee - eye, oh!
And on that farm he had a donkey,
Ee - eye, ee - eye, oh!
With a hee haw here
And a hee haw there.
Here a hee, there a haw,
Everywhere a hee haw.
Old MacDonald had a farm,
Ee - eye, ee - eye, oh!

Traditional

Marshmallow Rice Krispie Treats

50g (2oz) butter
200g (8oz) white marshmallows
150g (6oz) crispy rice cereal

Grease a 22 x 33cm (9inch x 13inch) tin with oil or butter.
Melt the butter in a large saucepan over a low heat, taking care not to burn it.
Add the vanilla.
Melt the marshmallows into the butter, stirring all the time.
When the marshmallows have melted add the cereal and stir until it is fully coated.
Pour the mixture into the prepared tin, and using a spatula, quickly and evenly press it out to all corners.
Leave for two to three hours to set.
Cut into pleasing cubes.

Toffee

You will need:
170ml (6fl oz) water
50g (2oz) butter
850g (2lb 2oz) brown sugar

Boil the water, sugar and butter in a pan.
Whilst hot, pour onto a buttered oven tray.
When cool, break into bite-size pieces.

Flapjack

125g (5oz) butter or margarine
100g (4oz) dark brown soft sugar
4 tablespoons golden syrup
250g (10oz) rolled oats
50g (2oz) sultanas or raisins (optional)
Preheat oven to 180°C/gas mark 4

In a saucepan, over a low heat, combine the butter, brown sugar and golden syrup.
Cook, stirring occasionally, until butter and sugar have melted.
Stir in the oats and sultanas until coated.
Pour into a 20cm square baking tin.
The mixture should be 2cm–3cm thick.
Bake for 30 minutes in the preheated oven, or until the top is golden.
Cut into squares, then leave to cool completely before removing from the tin.

one man went to mow

Verse 1
One man went to mow,
Went to mow a meadow.
One man and his dog
Went to mow a meadow.

Verse 2
Two men went to mow,
Went to mow a meadow.
Two men, one man and his dog
Went to mow a meadow.

Verse 3
Three men went to mow,
Went to mow a meadow.
Three men, two men, one man and his dog
Went to mow a meadow.

Verse 4
Four men went to mow,
Went to mow a meadow.
Four men, three men, two men, one man and his dog
Went to mow a meadow.

Verse 5
Five men went to mow,
Went to mow a meadow.
Five men, four men, three men, two men, one man and his dog
Went to mow a meadow.

Verse 6
Six men went to mow,
Went to mow a meadow.
Six men, five men, four men, three men, two men, one man and his dog
Went to mow a meadow.

Verse 7
Six men went to mow,
Went to mow a meadow.
Seven men, six men, five men, four men, three men, two men, one man and his dog
Went to mow a meadow.

Traditional

F
One man went to mow,

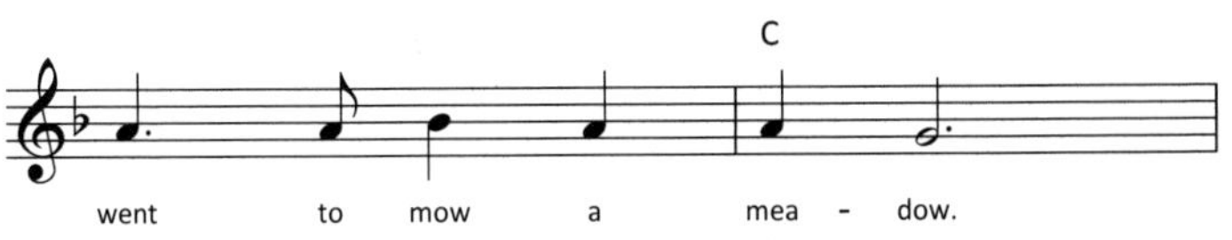
C
went to mow a mea - dow.

Repeat as necessary
C7
One man and his dog

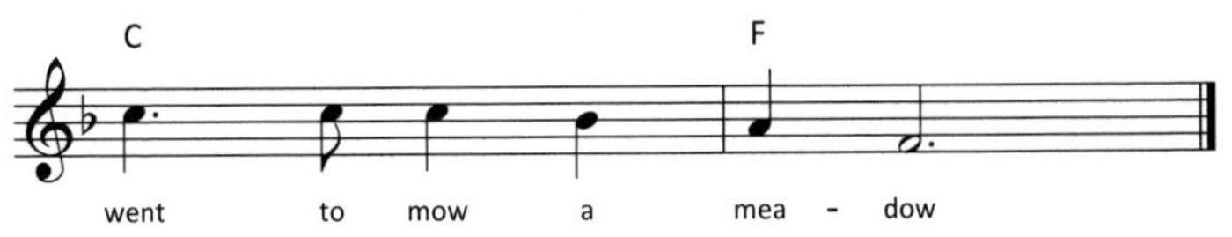
C
F
went to mow a mea - dow

the owl and the pussycat

Verse 1

The owl and the pussycat went to sea
In a beautiful peagreen boat;
They took some honey and plenty of money
Wrapped up in a five-pound note.

The owl looked up to the stars above
And sang to a small guitar,
"O, lovely Pussy, o Pussy my love,
What a beautiful Pussy you are,
You are, you are.
What a beautiful Pussy you are!"

Verse 2

Pussy said to the owl, "You elegant fowl,
How charmingly sweet you sing.
O, let us be married, too long we have tarried,
But what shall we do for a ring?"

They sailed away for a year and a day
To the land where the Bongtree grows.
And there in a wood a Piggywig stood
With a ring at the end of his nose,
His nose, his nose.
With a ring at the end of his nose.

Verse 3

"Dear Pig, are you willing to sell for one shilling your ring?"
Said the Piggy, "I will."
So they took it away and were married next day
By the turkey who lives on the hill.

They dined on mince and slices of quince
Which they ate with a runcible spoon;
And hand in hand on the edge of the sand
They danced by the light of the moon,
The moon, the moon.
They danced by the light of the moon.

Words by Edward Lear
Music by Victor Hely-Hutchinson

pop goes the weasel

Half a pound of tuppenny rice,
Half a pound of treacle,
That's the way the money goes,
Pop goes the weasel.

Traditional

D
A7
D
A7
Half a pound of tup- pen - ny rice, half a pound of

D
A7
D
trea - cle, that's the way the mon - ey goes,

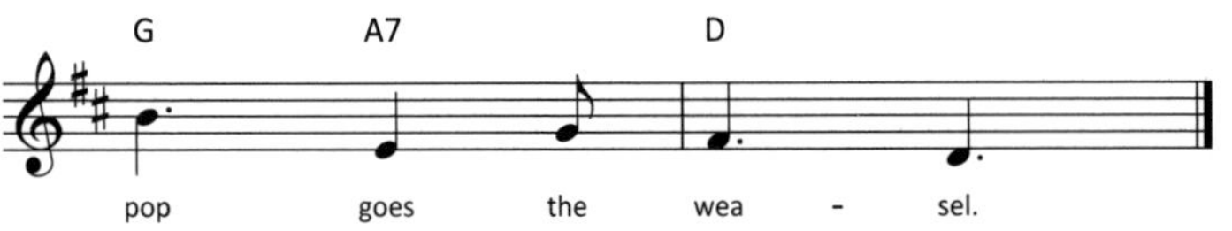
G
A7
D
pop goes the wea - sel.

row, row, row your boat

Row, row, row your boat,
Gently down the stream,
Merrily, merrily, merrily, merrily,
Life is but a dream.

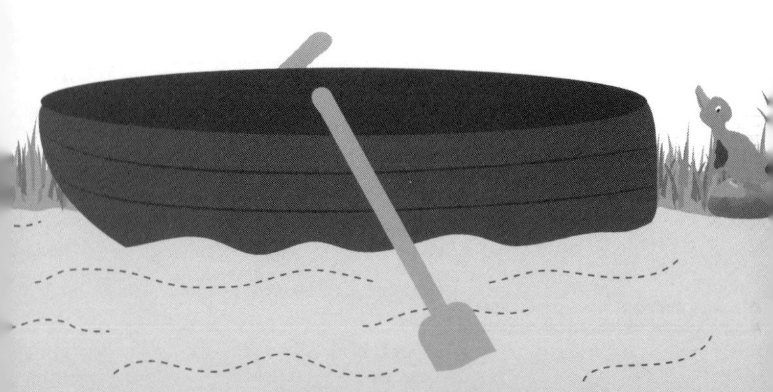

Traditional

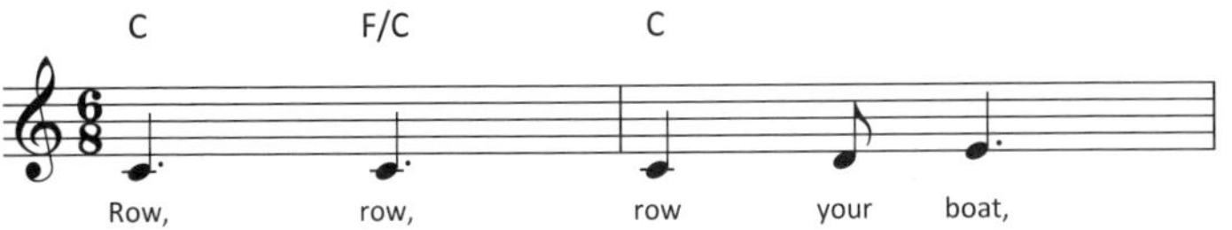

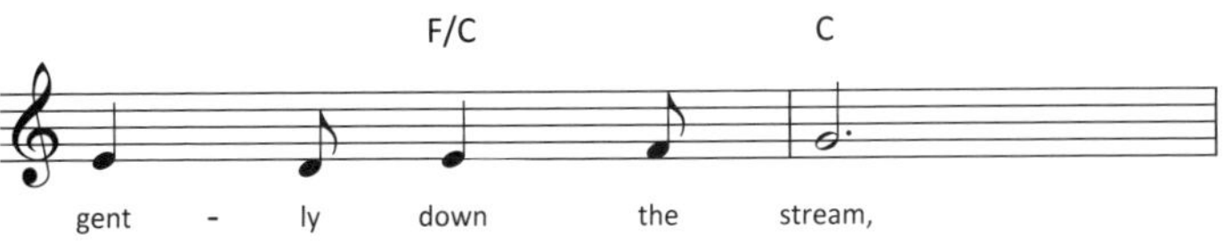

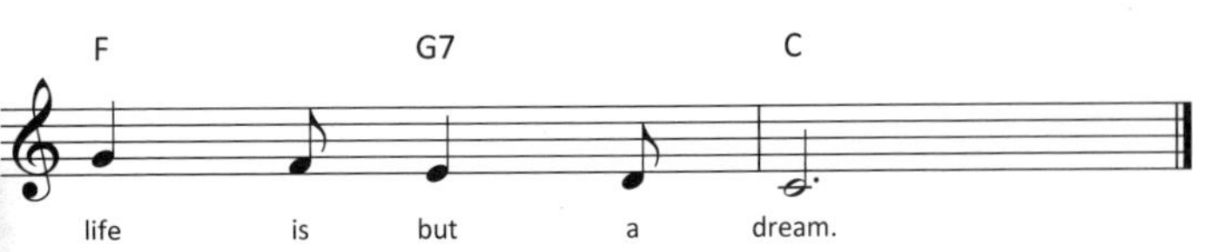

travel quotes

The World is a book, and those who do not travel read only a page.
– St. Augustine

The only way of catching a train I ever discovered is to miss the train before.
– G. K. Chesterton

I travel not to go anywhere, but to go. I travel for travel's sake. The great affair is to move.
– Robert Louis Stevenson

Travel and change of place impart new vigour to the mind.
– Seneca

A good traveller has no fixed plans, and is not intent on arriving.
– Lao Tzu

I have found out that there ain't no surer way to find out whether you like people or hate them than to travel with them.
– Mark Twain

The whole object of travel is not to set foot on foreign land;
it is at last to set foot on one's own country as a foreign land.
– G. K. Chesterton

Travel is fatal to prejudice, bigotry, and narrow-mindedness,
and many of our people need it sorely on these accounts.
Broad, wholesome, charitable views of men and things cannot be acquired
by vegetating in one little corner of the earth all one's lifetime.
– Mark Twain

The traveller sees what he sees.
The tourist sees what he has come to see.
– G. K. Chesterton

Like all great travellers, I have seen more than I remember,
and remember more than I have seen.
– Benjamin Disraeli

Voyage, travel, and change of place impart vigour.
– Seneca

Some roads aren't meant to be travelled alone.
– Proverb

Travel, in the younger sort, is a part of education;
in the elder, a part of experience.
– Francis Bacon

Journeys end in lovers meeting.
– Shakespeare

she'll be coming 'round the mountain

Verse 1

She'll be comin' 'round the mountain when she comes. (Yee-ha!)
She'll be comin' 'round the mountain when she comes. (Yee-ha!)
She'll be comin' 'round the mountain,
She'll be comin' 'round the mountain,
She'll be comin' 'round the mountain when she comes. (Yee-ha!)

Singin' eye eye yippee yippee eye,
Singin' eye eye yippee yippee eye,
Singin' eye eye yippee,
Eye eye yippee,
Eye eye yippee yippee eye.

Verse 2

She'll be ridin' six white horses when she comes. (Whoa back!)...

Singin' eye eye yippee yippee eye...

Verse 3

Oh we'll all come out to meet her when she comes. (Hi, babe!)...

Singin' eye eye yippee yippee eye...

Verse 4

She'll be wearin' pink pyjamas when she comes. (Wolf whistle)...

Singin' eye eye yippee yippee eye...

Verse 5

Oh we'll have to sleep with Grandma when she comes. (Snore snore!)...

Singin' eye eye yippee yippee eye...

Verse 6

Oh we'll all have chicken and dumplings when she comes. (Yum yum!)...

Singin' eye eye yippee yippee eye...

Verse 7

Oh we'll kill the old red rooster when she comes. (Chop chop!)...

Singin' eye eye yippee yippee eye...

Traditional

sing a song of sixpence

Verse 1
Sing a song of sixpence,
A pocket full of rye,
Four and twenty blackbirds
Baked in a pie.
When the pie was opened
The birds began to sing,
Wasn't that a dainty dish
To set before a King!

Verse 2
The King was in his counting house,
Counting out his money.
The Queen was in the parlour,
Eating bread and honey.
The maid was in the garden,
Hanging out the clothes,
When down came a blackbird
And pecked off her nose.

Traditional

ten green bottles

Verse 1
Ten green bottles hanging on the wall.
Ten green bottles hanging on the wall,
And if one green bottle should accidentally fall
There'll be nine green bottles hanging on the wall.

Verse 2
Nine green bottles hanging on the wall...

Verse 3
Eight green bottles hanging on the wall...

Verse 4
Seven green bottles hanging on the wall...

Verse 5
Six green bottles hanging on the wall...

Verse 6
Five green bottles hanging on the wall...

Verse 7
Four green bottles hanging on the wall...

Verse 8
Three green bottles hanging on the wall...

Verse 9
Two green bottles hanging on the wall...

Verse 10
One green bottle hanging on the wall.
One green bottle hanging on the wall,
And if that green bottle should accidentally fall
There'll be no green bottles hanging on the wall.

Traditional

F
C7
F
Ten green bot - tles___ hang - ing on the wall.

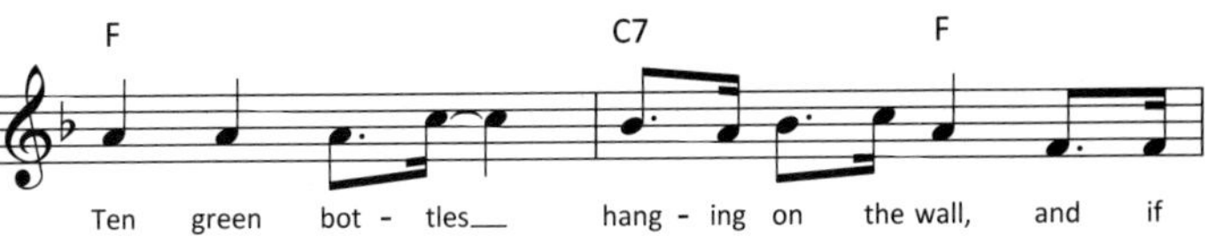
F
C7
F
Ten green bot - tles___ hang - ing on the wall, and if

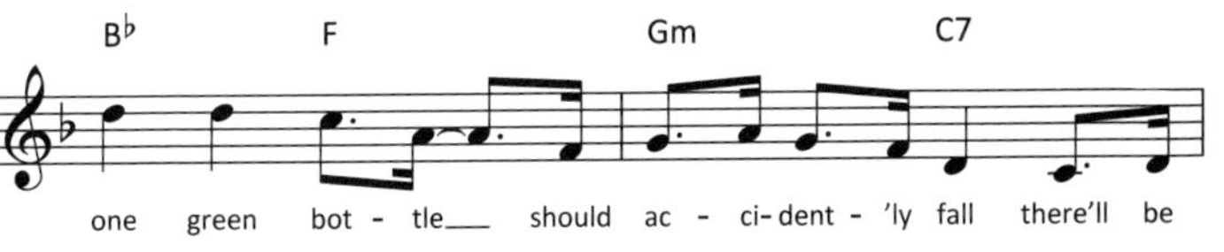
B♭
F
Gm
C7
one green bot - tle___ should ac - ci- dent - 'ly fall there'll be

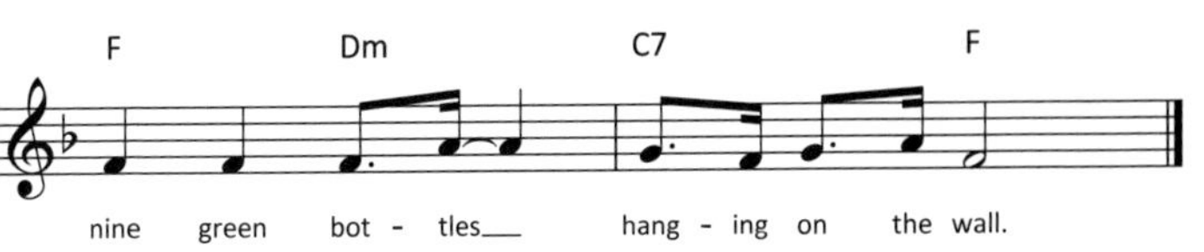
F
Dm
C7
F
nine green bot - tles___ hang - ing on the wall.

there's a hole in my bucket

Verse 1
There's a hole in my bucket, dear Liza, dear Liza,
There's a hole in my bucket, dear Liza, a hole.
Then fix it, dear Henry, dear Henry, dear Henry,
Then fix it, dear Henry, dear Henry, fix it.

Verse 2
With what shall I fix it, dear Liza, dear Liza?
With what shall I fix it, dear Liza, with what?
With some straw, dear Henry, dear Henry, dear Henry
With some straw, dear Henry, dear Henry, some straw

Verse 3
The straw is too long, dear Liza, dear Liza,
The straw is too long, dear Liza, too long.
Then cut it, dear Henry, dear Henry, dear Henry,
Then cut it, dear Henry, dear Henry, cut it.

Verse 4
With what shall I cut it, dear Liza, dear Liza?
With what shall I cut it, dear Liza, with what?
With an axe, dear Henry, dear Henry, dear Henry,
With an axe, dear Henry, dear Henry, an axe.

Verse 5
The axe is too dull, dear Liza, dear Liza,
The axe is too dull, dear Liza, too dull.
Then sharpen it, dear Henry, dear Henry, dear Henry,
Then sharpen it, dear Henry, dear Henry, sharpen it.

Verse 6
With what shall I sharpen it, dear Liza, dear Liza?
With what shall I sharpen it, dear Liza, with what?
With a stone, dear Henry, dear Henry, dear Henry,
With a stone, dear Henry, dear Henry, a stone.

Verse 7
The stone is too dry, dear Liza, dear Liza,
The stone is too dry, dear Liza, too dry.
Then moisten it, dear Henry, dear Henry, dear Henry,
Then moisten it, dear Henry, dear Henry, moisten it.

Verse 8
With what shall I moisten, dear Liza, dear Liza?
With what shall I moisten, dear Liza, with what?
Try water, dear Henry, dear Henry, dear Henry,
Try water, dear Henry, dear Henry, try water.

Verse 9
From where shall I get it, dear Liza, dear Liza?
From where shall I get it, dear Liza, from where?
From the well, dear Henry, dear Henry, dear Henry,
From the well, dear Henry, dear Henry, the well.

Verse 10
In what shall I fetch it, dear Liza, dear Liza?
In what shall I fetch it, dear Liza, in what?
In a bucket dear Henry, dear Henry, dear Henry,
In a bucket dear Henry, dear Henry, in a bucket.

You have the option to repeat the song, although it would go on for a long time!

Traditional

travel nonsense

The Pobble Who Has No Toes

By Edward Lear

The Pobble who has no toes
Had once as many as we;
When they said, “Some day you may lose them all.”
He replied “Fish, fiddle-de-dee!”
And his Aunt Jobiska made him drink
Lavender water tinged with pink,
For she said “The World in general knows
There’s nothing so good for a Pobble’s toes!”
The Pobble who has no toes
Swam across the Bristol Channel;
But before he set out he wrapped his nose
In a piece of scarlet flannel.
For his Aunt Jobiska said “No harm
Can come to his toes if his nose is warm;
And it’s perfectly known that a Pobble’s toes
Are safe, provided he minds his nose!”
The Pobble swam fast and well,
And when boats or ships came near him,
He tinkledy-blinkledy-winkled a bell,
So that all the world could hear him.

And all the Sailors and Admirals cried,
When they saw him nearing the further side,
"He has gone to fish for his Aunt Jobiska's
Runcible Cat with crimson whiskers!"
But before he touched the shore,
The shore of the Bristol Channel,
A sea-green porpoise carried away
His wrapper of scarlet flannel.
And when he came to observe his feet,
Formerly garnished with toes so neat,
His face at once became forlorn,
On perceiving that all his toes were gone!
And nobody ever knew,
From that dark day to the present,
Whoso had taken the Pobble's toes,
In a manner so far from pleasant.
Whether the shrimps, or crawfish grey,
Or crafty Mermaids stole them away.
Nobody knew: and nobody knows
How the Pobble was robbed of his twice five toes!
The Pobble who has no toes
Was placed in a friendly Bark,
And they rowed him back, and carried him up
To his Aunt Jobiska's Park.
And she made him a feast at his earnest wish
Of eggs and buttercups fried with fish,
And she said, "It's a fact the whole world knows,
That Pobbles are happier without their toes!"

there were ten in the bed

Verse 1
There were ten in the bed and the little one said,
"Roll over, roll over!"
So they all rolled over and one fell out.

Verse 2
There were nine in the bed and the little one said,
"Roll over, roll over!"
So they all rolled over and one fell out.

Verse 3
There were eight in the bed and the little one said,
"Roll over, roll over!"
So they all rolled over and one fell out.

Verse 4
There were seven in the bed and the little one said,
"Roll over, roll over!"
So they all rolled over and one fell out.

Verse 5
There were six in the bed and the little one said,
"Roll over, roll over!"
So they all rolled over and one fell out.

Verse 6
There were five in the bed and the little one said,
"Roll over, roll over!"
So they all rolled over and one fell out.

Verse 7
There were four in the bed and the little one said,
"Roll over, roll over!"
So they all rolled over and one fell out.

Verse 8
There were three in the bed and the little one said,
"Roll over, roll over!"
So they all rolled over and one fell out.

Verse 9
There were two in the bed and the little one said,
"Roll over, roll over!"
So they all rolled over and one fell out.

Verse 10
There was one in the bed and the little one said,
"GOOD NIGHT!"

Traditional

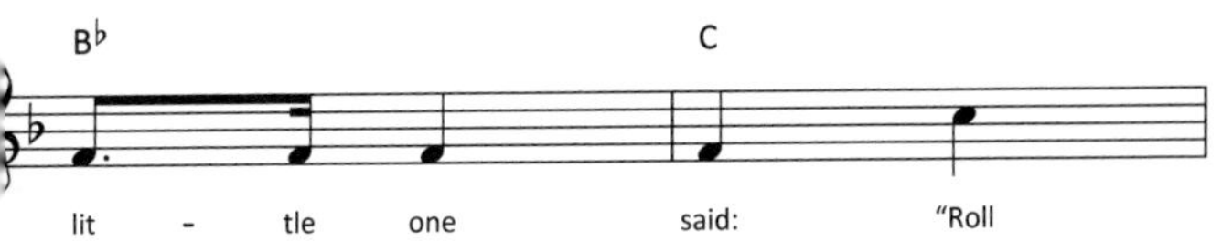

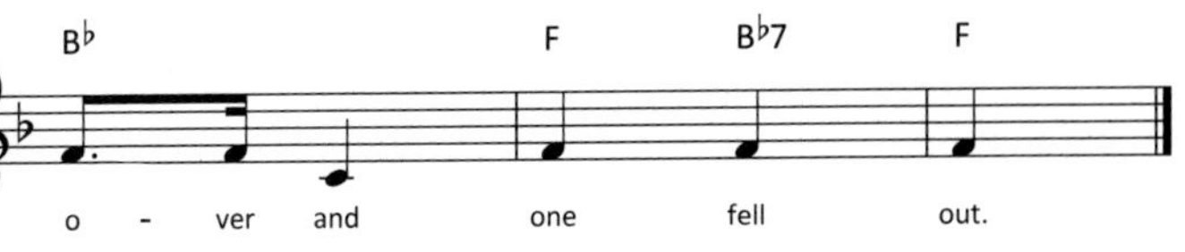

this old man

Verse 1
This old man, he played one,
He played knick-knack on my thumb,
With a knick-knack paddywhack,
Give a dog a bone,
This old man came rolling home.

Verse 2
This old man, he played two,
He played knick-knack on my shoe,
With a knick-knack paddywhack,
Give a dog a bone,
This old man came rolling home.

Verse 3
This old man, he played three,
He played knick-knack on my knee,
With a knick-knack paddywhack,
Give a dog a bone,
This old man came rolling home.

Verse 4
This old man, he played four,
He played knick-knack on my door,
With a knick-knack paddywhack,
Give a dog a bone,
This old man came rolling home.

Verse 5
This old man, he played five,
He played knick-knack on my hive,
With a knick-knack paddywhack,
Give a dog a bone,
This old man came rolling home.

Verse 6
This old man, he played six,
He played knick-knack on my sticks,
With a knick-knack paddywhack,
Give a dog a bone,
This old man came rolling home.

Verse 7
This old man, he played seven,
He played knick-knack up in Heaven,
With a knick-knack paddywhack,
Give a dog a bone,
This old man came rolling home.

Verse 8
This old man, he played eight,
He played knick-knack on my gate,
With a knick-knack paddywhack,
Give a dog a bone,
This old man came rolling home.

Verse 9
This old man, he played nine,
He played knick-knack on my spine,
With a knick-knack paddywhack,
Give a dog a bone,
This old man came rolling home.

Verse 10
This old man, he played ten,
He played knick-knack once again,
With a knick-knack paddywhack,
Give a dog a bone,
This old man came rolling home.

Traditional

C
This old man, he played one,

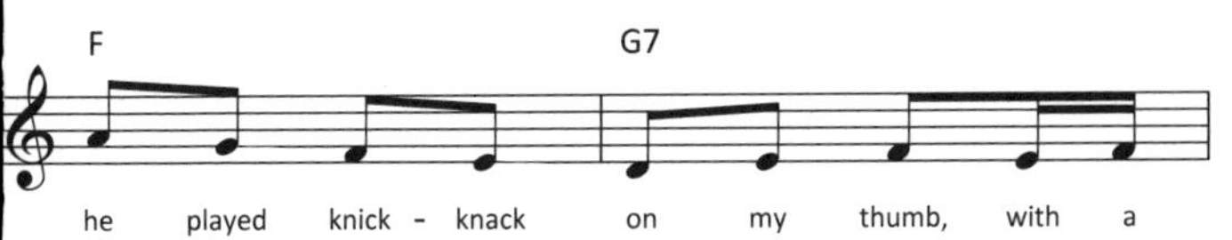
F
G7
he played knick - knack on my thumb, with a

C
Am
G
knick - knack pad - dy whack give a dog a bone,

G7
C
this old man came roll - ing home.

three blind mice

Three blind mice,
Three blind mice.
See how they run!
See how they run!
They all ran after the farmer's wife,
Who cut off their tails with a carving knife,
Did ever you see such a thing in your life,
As three blind mice?

Traditional

the wheels on the bus

Verse 1

The wheels on the bus go round and round,
Round and round, round and round.
The wheels on the bus go round and round,
All day long.

Verse 2

The wipers on the bus go swish, swish, swish,
Swish, swish, swish, swish, swish, swish.
The wipers on the bus go swish, swish, swish,
All day long.

Verse 3

The horn on the bus goes beep, beep, beep,
Beep, beep, beep, beep, beep, beep.
The horn on the bus goes beep, beep, beep,
All day long.

Verse 4

The children on the bus go chatter, chatter, chatter,
Chatter, chatter, chatter, chatter, chatter, chatter.
The children on the bus go chatter, chatter, chatter,
All day long.

Verse 5

The people on the bus bounce up and down,
Up and down, up and down.
The people on the bus bounce up and down,
All day long.

Verse 6

The babies on the bus fall fast asleep,
Fast asleep, fast asleep.
The babies on the bus fall fast asleep,
All day long.

Traditional

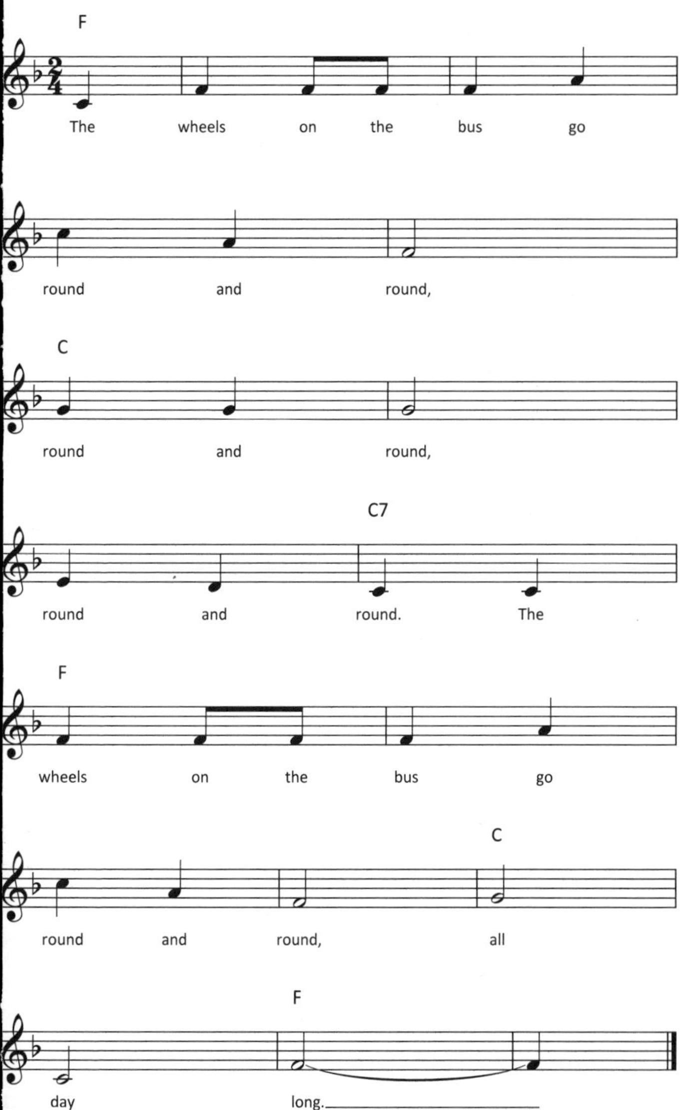

ENJOY HOURS OF FUN WITH THESE GREAT GAMES...

Pop The Question ®

Test family and friends with these fantastic trivia games & find out who is the biggest music fan of all!

Pop The Question	GAM1287
Pop The Question Extra	GAM1683
More Pop The Question	GAM1309
More Pop The Question Extra	GAM1694
Pop The Question Rock	GAM1320
Pop The Question Rock Extra	GAM1705
Pop The Question Soul, Funk & Hip-Hop	GAM1331
Pop The Question Soul, Funk & Hip-Hop Extra	GAM1716
Pop The Question 50s & 60s	GAM1342
Pop The Question 50s & 60s Extra	GAM1727
Pop The Question 70s & 80s	GAM1353
Pop The Question 70s & 80s Extra	GAM1738

Popdoku

Customers will love this upbeat Sudoku game with a musical twist. Players test their speed of thought and powers of deduction to place Kylie, Elton and Robbie in the correct line-up. Great fun at Christmastime.

GAM1430

Toonology

Mind benders with a musical twist! Players test their musical knowledge and powers of deduction by unravelling the hilarious 'Toons'.

GAM1133